School Days

Twenty Poems from the Classroom

Candlestick Press

Published by:
Candlestick Press,
Diversity House, 72 Nottingham Road, Arnold, Nottingham NG5 6LF
www.candlestickpress.co.uk

Design and typesetting by Craig Twigg

Printed by Bayliss Printing Company Ltd of Worksop, UK

Selections and Introductions © Jeanette Burton and Jonathan Edwards, 2024

Cover illustration © Cat Moore, 2024
https://www.catmooreprintmaker.co.uk/

Candlestick Press monogram © Barbara Shaw, 2008

© Candlestick Press, 2024

ISBN 978 1 913627 43 0

Contents
Page

Ten Poems about School

Ten Poems about Teachers

Ten Poems about School

Introduction

When I was in school, we had a DT teacher – Mr Harries – who used to say a very strange thing. He'd stand there, tapping a hacksaw against a piece of wood or tightening plastic into a vice, and solemnly announce it to the class. "School days," he'd say, "are the best days of your life".

For all us ragamuffins, it was a sentence beyond comprehension, and caused us to conclude that either Mr Harries's post-school life had been extremely boring, or that decades of standing too near the fumes of the soldering iron had marred his thinking. Now though, I'm not so sure: as the years pass, as memories become mythologies, I find myself smiling at the outright craziness of those days.

So here's a pamphlet for Mr Harries – and hopefully for you! – to celebrate the rich range of things school gives us. Chief among these, of course, is the people it brings us into contact with. Charles Causley's 'Timothy Winters' makes a social point by giving us an unforgettable individual, and it's answered here by Hannah Lowe, who gives us an equally memorable character.

Ideas of schooling – what is school for? – can have as many variations as there are people on the planet. Thomas Lux protests how education can be pointed towards money and away from creativity, while Jennifer Wong celebrates the heroism of village schools in China, where education leads pupils "to a place they imagine".

Perhaps the greatest of school's treasures though is its sense of discovery, and this collection ends with poems by Mary Ruefle and Denise Duhamel, which celebrate education's daily breakthroughs, in knowing the world and knowing ourselves.

Who'd have thought that schools could contain so much, that they could contain the whole world? I know by now I'll never in this life stand before a class with a hacksaw, expounding the virtues of education. Yet here I am, reader, gathering all these poems in this pamphlet, brushing something – is that sawdust? – from the cover, and handing them to you.

Jonathan Edwards

The Hand

The teacher asks a question.
You know the answer, you suspect
you are the only one in the classroom
who knows the answer, because the person
in question is yourself, and on that
you are the greatest living authority,
but you don't raise your hand.
You raise the top of your desk
and take out an apple.
You look out the window.
You don't raise your hand and there is
some essential beauty in your fingers,
which aren't even drumming, but lie
flat and peaceful.
The teacher repeats the question.
Outside the window, on an overhanging branch,
a robin is ruffling its feathers
and spring is in the air.

Mary Ruefle

Timothy Winters

Timothy Winters comes to school
With eyes as wide as a football-pool,
Ears like bombs and teeth like splinters:
A blitz of a boy is Timothy Winters.

His belly is white, his neck is dark,
And his hair is an exclamation-mark.
His clothes are enough to scare a crow
And through his britches the blue winds blow.

When teacher talks he won't hear a word
And he shoots down dead the arithmetic-bird,
He licks the patterns off his plate
And he's not even heard of the Welfare State.

Timothy Winters has bloody feet
And he lives in a house on Suez Street,
He sleeps in a sack on the kitchen floor
And they say there aren't boys like him any more.

Old Man Winters likes his beer
And his missus ran off with a bombardier,
Grandma sits in the grate with a gin
And Timothy's dosed with an aspirin.

The Welfare Worker lies awake
But the law's as tricky as a ten-foot snake,
So Timothy Winters drinks his cup
And slowly goes on growing up.

At Morning Prayers the Master helves
For children less fortunate than ourselves,
And the loudest response in the room is when
Timothy Winters roars 'Amen!'

So come one angel, come on ten:
Timothy Winters says 'Amen
Amen amen amen amen.'
Timothy Winters, Lord.

                            Amen.

Charles Causley (1917 – 2003)

Simile

Timothy Winters has ears like bombs and teeth like splinters...

I can't remember when, or which old teacher
chalked Charles Causley's words on the board, glued them
onto my brain, so whenever I need to remember
or explain what 'simile' is, I use that poem –
poor Timothy Winters with his meagre face
though really, all these years, it's Bobbi, a girl
from school that I've been seeing. Bobbi, who'd chase
and kiss any boy with her ragged, gaping smile,

scuttling the asphalt in her too small skirts
and a galaxy of moon-shaped plasters peeling
from her neck and shoulders. Nobody liked her.
But nowadays to think of Bobbi hurts
like a fading bruise you keep on poking.
Bobbi Bonniwell. What happened to her?

Hannah Lowe

How It All Started

Do you know this dream? An exam room
full of neat, serious girls, your lucky gonk
by your fountain pen, the plop of tennis balls
through an open window. You're here for
'O' level history on The Causes
Of The First World War but you've no idea –
too busy bunking off to watch *Crown Court*,
and the teacher says *You may turn over*
and begin and there's a question
on the Algeciras crisis and all you can think is,
Algeciras sounds like a virus or a cloud formation,
your eyes blur, scanning for something
you understand, you wonder who Bismarck was,
why his web of Alliances was so significant,
your throat swells like a new loaf, you watch
the girls who know the answers to these things,
and you think of the stutter of gunfire, a soldier's
booted foot lying in a puddle, how the leather split,
how the rest of him wasn't there, just a stump
of bone, and if you'd learned how it all started,
you might have known how to prevent this.
You should have known how to prevent this.

Catherine Smith

You Go to School to Learn

You go to school to learn to
read and add, to someday
make some money. It—money—makes
sense: you need
a better tractor, an addition
to the gameroom, you prefer
to buy your beancurd by the barrel.
There's no other way to get the goods
you need. Besides, it keeps people busy
working—for it.
It's sensible and, therefore, you go
to school to learn (and the teacher,
having learned, gets paid to teach you) how
to get it. Fine. But:
you're taught away from poetry
or, say, dancing (*That's nice, dear,
but there's no dough in it*). No poem
ever bought a hamburger, or not too many. It's true,
and so, every morning—it's still dark!—
you see them, the children, like angels
being marched off to execution,
or banks. Their bodies luminous
in headlights. Going to school.

Thomas Lux (1946 – 2017)

Small School

Since Project Hope began in 1989, over 15000 village schools have been built in China.

They get dressed in pre-dawn darkness. For hours they'd follow a path only they know, around them no signposts, only mountains. Quarry, sand in the wind, and wild slopes.

Every step is a step away from home, leads them to a place they imagine, and the sky slowly fills with light.

The building is so plain you won't notice. No name. No heating. Just a room with haphazard stools and desks. Dust falling eternally on curtainless windows. At noon, they queue on the playground for hard-boiled eggs and steamed rice, or a turn to play the battered piano. The water they drink comes from a well one kilometre away. Each day, the chef goes there to fetch water on his motorbike.

Six thousand miles from where I am – on Guizhou's darkening mountains – these silhouettes in twos and threes who keep walking, fearless soldiers of the weather, carrying their satchels and tiny torches of hope.

Jennifer Wong

Re-enactment of the Chartist March, Waunfawr Primary School, Crosskeys, Spring 1991

The day we dressed up
in Dai caps, bits and pieces, this
and that, our uncles' waistcoats, knitted
shawls, whatever our parents could lay
their hands on, the day we stood shoulder
to shoulder to have our photos taken, what
were we, eleven, but suddenly little
old men, old ladies, children's eyes looking out
from under clothes so ill-fitting, so out
of time, it was like they wore us. The day

you'd planned for a year, the day we set out,
carrying the placards you'd shown us
how to make, the ones with the words
you gave us: *Secret ballot. Votes for all men
over 21.* The lessons where you told us
what *Suffrage* meant, and we tried the word
in our mouths, found it big as a stone. The day

we walked out, down the road, a fearsome
crew, demanding our rights, while volunteer
parents shouted *Stay on the kerb!* We walked
into the past, from here to there, now
to then, and when I think of it I don't know
how we did it, all that way, Crosskeys
to Rogerstone, what, five miles, our little legs,
weighed down by clothes and history, mile
by mile feeling what they did. At the end,

we sat on benches outside The Welsh Oak,
where they met, where you'd arranged for squash
and sandwiches, and the man from the local
Chartist association told us the things
you already had, not as well as you had, not
in your voice. Three years

and you'd be dead, and when my mother
went to visit you in hospital, you said you'd never
done anything you wanted in this life. That day
outside The Welsh Oak, you sat
on a picnic bench in the sun, and the sky
stayed dry for you, Mrs B, and if I could, what I'd do now

is step back to that day: I'd walk up to you, and tell you
to take a good look round, to really look
at everything you gave us, all us kids, in borrowed clothes
we'll try for years to grow into – words, a past, a ragged
sense of self. And I'd tell you how this day will sing

all through a life, how it's still there now, I can reach out
and touch it whenever I need it, and how you
did all of this, Mrs B, how you did everything.

Jonathan Edwards

After Lessons

The classrooms are as dead as winter trees.
You hold your breath along the corridor –
Your plimsolls creak. There is no other noise.

A single light ices the polished floor.
You turn and, somehow, end up in The Boys,
A row of basins level with your knees.

You shouldn't be inside this place so late.
I wonder what you thought you might achieve
By squinting at the blackboard. What, and how?

In the dark, you wipe your nose across your sleeve.
It's much too late to put your hand up now.
There's someone outside, waiting at the gate.

Stephen Knight

Homeric

Like a schoolboy groping for a marble
in his jacket pocket while the teacher
prattles on at the front of the class,
then smuggling it in his clammy fist
to the hole in the top right corner of his desk,
redundant now, but where in olden days
an inkwell would have rested snugly,
then opening his fist to let the marble
drop as noiselessly as possible before
trickling down the complicated chute
secretly and patiently constructed
from books, their foredges turned upwards,
riskily balanced rulers, bits of rubbish
found around the school grounds,
while he follows in his imagination
its devious descent through a darkness
redolent of old wood, dust and pencil shavings
till it reaches the hole in the base of the desk –
the purpose of which can only be
this furtive and thrilling game –
where all this time his other hand
has been waiting to catch and pocket it...

Christopher Reid

Ego

I just didn't get it—
even with the teacher holding an orange (the earth) in one hand
and a lemon (the moon) in the other,
her favorite student (the sun) standing behind her with a flashlight.
I just couldn't grasp it—
this whole citrus universe, these bumpy planets revolving so slowly
no one could even see themselves moving.
I used to think if I could only concentrate hard enough
I could be the one person to feel what no one else could,
sense a small tug from the ground, a sky shift, the earth changing gears.
Even though I was only one mini-speck on a speck,
even though I was merely a pinprick in one goosebump on the orange,
I was sure then I was the most specially perceptive, perceptively sensitive.
I was sure then my mother was the only mother to snap,
"The world doesn't revolve around you!"
The earth was fragile and mostly water,
just the way the orange was mostly water if you peeled it,
just the way I was mostly water if you peeled me.
Looking back on that third grade science demonstration,
I can understand why some people gave up on fame or religion or cures—
especially people who have an understanding
of the excruciating crawl of the world,
who have a well-developed sense of spatial reasoning
and the tininess that it is to be one of us.
But not me—even now I wouldn't mind being god, the force
who spins the planets the way I spin a globe, a basketball, a yoyo.
I wouldn't mind being that teacher who chooses the fruit,
or that favorite kid who gives the moon its glow.

Denise Duhamel

Ten Poems about Teachers

Introduction

As an English teacher, I'm pretty sure I'm not alone in being
inspired by the charismatic Mr Keating from *Dead Poets Society*.
Who doesn't want to stand on a desk, quote Whitman, transform
young lives with new perspectives? Such wondrous, maverick
beings also exist in the real world. Mr Stephenson, my primary
school teacher, had an extraordinary ability to mesmerise with
his singing and comedy routines. The poems in this anthology
celebrate these incredible figures, but they also explore the reality
of the education system. Teaching is rarely as dynamic as a
Hollywood movie, rather, as Andrew Jamison wistfully observes,
it often involves bearing witness to the endless procession of
students, marching themselves into the future, leaving us behind.

Kathryn Bevis's poem is a powerful testament to the challenges
teachers face daily, not only from inspections, assessment, rigid
standards, but also from the dire socio-economic circumstances
endured by so many children in our schools. We are reminded that
teachers fulfil a variety of roles, and that empathy is not easily
measured by league tables. Kim Moore follows a similar theme in
her wry and playful poem, 'Dear Mr Gove', championing music
as part of the creative arts and acknowledging that learning can be
worthwhile and joyful, even if it doesn't tick the right boxes.

Despite the ceaseless chug of the exam factory and government
initiatives, what all these poems have in common is their
humanity. Teaching is a humane profession. Somewhere beyond
the curriculum, the best teachers offer compassion, life lessons,
make dreams come true. Contrary to the stern, monolithic, head-
as-big-as-a-planet, schoolmaster of Oliver Goldsmith's poem,
Lorna Goodison's 'My Teacher Lena' proves the old adage true:
you never forget a good teacher, particularly one who encourages
you to find your own voice. Mr Stephenson and Mr Keating
would agree. *Carpe Diem!*

Jeanette Burton

.

Today, my students tell me

Today, my students tell me that I look like someone
who never drives a car, that I look like I am someone
who takes a train everywhere, and I love that they see me
like this, the same way that I love that one day, a student
asks me, do you buy your clothes on english teacher
dot com?, when the truth is, I would if such a place
existed. Another day, a student tells me that I seem
like the kind of person who is good at tending plants,
that I seem exactly like someone who would care for
dying plants and maybe even heal them, only I am the one
adding *maybe*, because they said it with such conviction
and another student agreed with them like this was simple
and true, and I laughed, told them they were wrong, that I wish
I were more like my grandmother, who was in fact a tender of gardens
and all green things and what I don't tell my students is that I
am so bad at taking care of anything including myself, I don't tell them
that their words, their kindness unprovoked by anything —
like when a student told me I smelled like waffles and they wanted
me to know this was a compliment — this tenderness, even just this shared
nodding of heads, that it takes care of me every day, that it keeps me like
                                                                    a garden.

Carla Sofia Ferreira

School Gates

is Matilda and Martha's favourite game.
They can play it for hours. It goes like this.
I have to be the teacher by the French window,
while they take it in turns to be the mother
dropping her daughter off and picking her up.
Nothing happens in between.
Just the meeting and the parting. Dropping off
is the hard bit, whoever's being mother
brings her daughter in, hangs up her school bag,
leaves her with her snack, takes teacher aside
and tells her it's a headache today
or she's been up in the night with earache
and might have to be picked up early.
The snack is a plastic carrot or a pepper
then it's time for the bell and the mother
runs in, arms open wide, hugs her child
and they stand for a while like that.
Then it's morning and the whole thing
starts again. Being a teacher's a piece of cake.

Carole Bromley

The Village School Master

Beside yon straggling fence that skirts the way
With blossom'd furze unprofitably gay,
There, in his noisy mansion, skill'd to rule,
The village master taught his little school;
A man severe he was, and stern to view,
I knew him well, and every truant knew;
Well had the boding tremblers learn'd to trace
The day's disasters in his morning face;
Full well they laugh'd with counterfeited glee,
At all his jokes, for many a joke had he:
Full well the busy whisper, circling round,
Convey'd the dismal tidings when he frown'd:
Yet he was kind; or if severe in aught,
The love he bore to learning was in fault.
The village all declar'd how much he knew;
'Twas certain he could write, and cipher too:
Lands he could measure, terms and tides presage,
And e'en the story ran that he could gauge.
In arguing too, the parson own'd his skill,
For e'en though vanquish'd he could argue still;
While words of learned length and thund'ring sound
Amazed the gazing rustics rang'd around;
And still they gaz'd and still the wonder grew,
That one small head could carry all he knew.
But past is all his fame. The very spot
Where many a time he triumph'd is forgot.

Oliver Goldsmith (1728 – 1774)

Miss means both *Mother* and *No-one*

The trainee teacher is crying in the loo. This time, for both intensity and duration, she has achieved *Outstanding*. And it's not Jed Simmonds or bottom-set Year Nine on Fridays, period five. It's not the safeguarding training or differentiation six ways for every class. She isn't crying for the Year Ten girls whose names she struggles to remember, so well have they hidden themselves behind long hair, immaculate behaviour, and precisely average grades. The trainee teacher is crying in the loo, her heart a strip-lit cubicle whose bulb is on the blink. And it's not her failure to meet sub-point 4d of the Teachers' Standards that's set her off on this occasion, nor is it the School Uniform Policy or the two-hundred-and-twenty-three books she has to mark each fortnight with rainbow highlighters, colour-coded for feedback, action, and response. The trainee teacher is crying in the loo, her heart a plug of chewing gum sticking to her ribs. She's not crying about the spreadsheets in which she must evidence two sub-levels of expected progress for each pupil, regardless of the child. She's not crying for the boy who mimicked fingering her when her back was to the class, nor for the Head who doesn't know her name. The trainee teacher is crying in the loo, her heart wrung and stinking as the mouldy mophead there's no budget to replace. She cries for let's-call-him Jaydon, Ahmed, Tom, held in isolation for a week because he threw a chair when his dad's parole date was postponed, cries for let's-call-her Aisha, Kayla, Kim, who cuts and cuts and shows her all the wounds, cries for the shrug of the Designated Safeguarding Lead (who's heard far worse than this today), for the twelve-year-olds who can't yet read, for the school-to-prison pipeline, for let's-call-him Connor, Kristos, Mo, slumped forever on the tutting chair outside the Head of Year.

Kathryn Bevis (1975 – 2024)

My Teacher Lena

They say – I'm not sure – that she now lives in a castle in Denmark.
Surely hers is a medieval castle with stone walls yards deep.
I visited Sweden in 1990 during the summer solstice.
The windows were blindless; the sun would not set.
I attempted to outstare it.

And I dined on schools of herring and small boiled potatoes
blue-white like opals and bought in a market, a paper bag
of cherries I ate all at one go as I sat on a park bench
to meditate upon Hans Christian Andersen
as played by Danny Kaye.

When I cobblestoned my way back to the bed and breakfast
where I stayed it had turned into a brick box of scandal
as the teenaged daughter of the owner – who was away
on vacation – decided to run off with
her mother's boyfriend.

He of the sad countenance and the ten-month pregnant paunch
whose hair was sparse; it was all very Ingmar Bergman.
While I was there I thought I'd go visit my teacher
in her castle; because in my atlas, Denmark
and Sweden are twinned

hence I'd be able to skip briskly across a fjord of connecting ice.
But the teenaged mess of a girl inside me blubbered how
she might not remember the overweight sixth former
who told her I wanted to read books with characters
who looked and sounded more like me.

And she'd said, 'You are a writer; write what you want to read.'

Lorna Goodison

Dear Mr Gove

dear Mr Gove today I taught the children not to sit like bags of small potatoes in their chairs I taught them how to breathe with their bellies like babies do when they are sleeping we pretended we were balloons of different colours filling up with air dear Mr Gove we played *long note beat that* we looked up who holds the world record for the longest note it was a clarinet player who managed to play for one minute and thirteen seconds without taking a breath we held our notes as if we were monks singing a drone in a cathedral where the roof rises like a giant wing against the sky dear Mr Gove today the whole class played hot cross buns we talked about the great height of the note E we held thin blue straws between our lips and some of us went on to play an E and some of us fell towards a low A with its ledger line hovering above it and another piercing its poor head dear Mr Gove we are brilliant at trying some of us know what crotchets and minims are and we will know this all our lives but some of us still call them black and white notes we make up sayings to help us read like Elephants Go Bananas Doing Flips like Electric Green Brains Dance Forever we play the riff to Eye of The Tiger and sing along in the voices of tigers if tigers had voices like ours today Mrs Johnson forgot how to play a D and Harry told her which valves to press I do not know how to measure this Mr Gove please send help and there is also the problem of Matthew who cannot read or write too well but who can play Mary Had A Little Lamb with perfect pitch there is the problem of his smile afterwards and how we write this down today we watched the muppets singing Bohemian Rhapsody for no good reason other than that it was fun and while I am confessing small transgressions last week we watched Mr Bean play an invisible drum kit the children have been playing an invisible drum kit in the playground dear Mr Gove I did not stop them today we talked about the muscles in the lip and tongue we did not know we had control of so many muscles we tried to look like musicians Mr Gove please help us

Kim Moore

Statement of Teaching Philosophy

My students want certainty. They want it
so badly. They respect science and have memorized
complex formulas. I don't know
how to tell my students their parents
are still just as scared. The bullies get bigger
and vaguer and you cannot punch a cloud.
I have eulogies for all my loved ones prepared,
but cannot include this fact in my lesson plans.
The best teacher I ever had told me to meet him
at the basketball court. We played pick-up for hours.
By the end, I lay panting on the hardwood
and couldn't so much as stand.
He told me to describe the pain in my chest.
I tried. I couldn't find the words. Not exactly.
Listen, he said, *that's where language ends*.

Keith Leonard

Teaching Keats' *La Belle Dame Sans Merci* on a Friday afternoon

We're just about coping with the concept
of pathetic fallacy at 4pm, last lesson,
and it's all decay and withering sedge.

What the hell is sedge, miss? I tell them we'll
talk about vegetation later, once we've dealt
with the tricky shorter line, the one that breaks

the rhythm of the ballad. *And no birds sing*,
offers a conscientious girl at the front,
of course, it mirrors the death of the knight.

A boy, the one who never takes his coat off,
but is always up for debate, likes to hit
assessment objective No 5 with alternative

interpretations, says, *He's just bloody hanging
around the hillside – like, is he dead or what?
Did that fairy-witch-girl-thing kill him, miss?*

Why doesn't he just chill out, let it go?
Good point, I think, but then realise how
easily these kids let things go, exiting

the classroom without a backward glance,
off into the weekend as if me, lessons,
college never existed. How completely

themselves they are. I'm tempted to say
I know something about limbo, being stuck.
No, not sojourning on the cold hill's side,

but carrying work, the building, on my back.
The difficulty I have driving down the motorway,
the whir of the staffroom on my shoulders,

the car packed to the gunnels with emails,
essays, reports, PowerPoints. All the chatter,
the talk of learning walks, Ofsted, steams up

the windows. I wipe away the latest meeting
minutes from the rear-view mirror, shut
a member of SLT in the glove compartment.

The boot bustles with the learning support team,
exams officers, pushing at the back seat
with desks, clocks, requests for spare books,

paper, extra time, someone to scribe. Estates
build a make-shift roof rack with whiteboards,
dodgy window clasps, see-through blinds.

Curled up in my left ear, the head of sixth form
whispers to me like a shell, not of the sea,
but of results, interventions, upcoming appraisal.

In my right ear, the tinnitus of a teenager's
repeated, *What is the task? What is the task?*
Each day, I'm hitched to this load, like Atlas,

my arms reaching behind me to hold the weight.
I wonder that the students never notice,
but close observation is not yet in their skill set,

racing ahead past the princes, kings, pale warriors,
closing the anthology with carefree fingers,
leaving the knight, loitering, on the cold hill's side.

Jeanette Burton

What You Missed That Day You Were Absent from Fourth Grade

Mrs. Nelson explained how to stand still and listen
to the wind, how to find meaning in pumping gas,

how peeling potatoes can be a form of prayer. She took
questions on how not to feel lost in the dark.

After lunch she distributed worksheets
that covered ways to remember your grandfather's

voice. Then the class discussed falling asleep
without feeling you had forgotten to do something else—

something important—and how to believe
the house you wake in is your home. This prompted

Mrs. Nelson to draw a chalkboard diagram detailing
how to chant the Psalms during cigarette breaks,

and how not to squirm for sound when your own thoughts
are all you hear; also, that you have enough.

The English lesson was that *I am*
is a complete sentence.

And just before the afternoon bell, she made the math equation
look easy. The one that proves that hundreds of questions,

and feeling cold, and all those nights spent looking
for whatever it was you lost, and one person

add up to something.

Brad Aaron Modlin

Teaching English

Hollywood would have us ripping introductions
clean from canonical anthologies, on tables
shouting *O Captain! My Captain!*, recitals interspersed
with penalty shootouts, secret midnight meetings
underground, smoking pipes and playing sax in berets,
giving lifts to troubled students on mopeds,
breaking into song mid close analysis in bow ties,
leather jackets, like jukeboxes of quotations.

Waiting at the whiteboard of my white-walled room
I've watched a squirrel and sunlight disappear
on the grass all day. All day they come and go:
a blur of blazers, red books, set texts, daydream,
and clock-watching. I give them what I know;
they pass down the corridor, into tomorrow.

Andrew Jamison

Acknowledgements

The poems in this pamphlet are reprinted from the following books, all by permission of the publishers listed unless stated otherwise. Every effort has been made to trace the copyright holders of the poems published in this book. The editors and publisher apologise if any material has been included without permission, or without the appropriate acknowledgement, and would be glad to be told of anyone who has not been consulted.

Thanks are due to all the copyright holders cited below for their kind permission.

Kathryn Bevis, *Flamingo* (Seren Books, 2022) by kind permission of the author and publisher. Carole Bromley, *The Stonegate Devil* (Smith/Doorstop, 2015) by kind permission of the author. Jeanette Burton, poem first appeared in this pamphlet. Charles Causley, *Collected Poems 1951-2000* (Picador, 2000). Denise Duhamel, *Queen for a Day: Selected & New Poems* (Pitt Poetry Series, 2001) reprinted by permission of The University of Pittsburgh Press. Jonathan Edwards, poem first appeared in this pamphlet. Carla Sofia Ferreira, *A Geography That Does Not Hurt Us* (River River Books, 2024) by kind permission of the author. Lorna Goodison, *Lorna Goodison: Collected Poems* (Carcanet Press, 2017). Andrew Jamison, *Swans We Cannot See* (Gallery Press, 2023). By kind permission of the author and The Gallery Press, Loughcrew, Oldcastle, County Meath, Ireland. Stephen Knight, *Dream City Cinema* (Bloodaxe Books, 1996) www.bloodaxebooks.com. Keith Leonard, *Waxwing Literary Journal*, issue 23, Spring 2021, by kind permission of the author. Hannah Lowe, *Kids* (Bloodaxe Books, 2021) www.bloodaxebooks.com. Thomas Lux, *New & Selected Poems of Thomas Lux: 1975-1995* (HarperCollins, 1999) by permission of Abner Stein Agency. Brad Aaron Modlin, *Everyone at This Party Has Two Names* (Southeast Missouri State University, 2016) by kind permission of the author. Kim Moore, *The Art of Falling* (Seren Books, 2015). Christopher Reid, *Toys/Tricks/Traps* (Faber & Faber, 2023) by permission of the publisher and Rogers, Coleridge & White Agency. Mary Ruefle, *Cold Pluto*. Copyright © 1996 by Mary Ruefle. Reprinted with the permission of The Permissions Company, LLC on behalf of Carnegie Mellon University Press, www.cmu.edu/universitypress. Catherine Smith, *Lip* (Smith|Doorstop, 2007).

All permissions cleared courtesy of Dr Suzanne Fairless-Aitken – Swift Permissions swiftpermissions@gmail.com.

Where poets are no longer living, their dates are given.